# PRAISE FOR GET CLIENTS FAST

## Helen Gets You Fired Up to Close More Deals

—◈◈◈—

"Ok, this is beautiful!  Common sense, straight talking, very clear and will resonate with anyone who has to get their own clients through the door. Helen's book is my new bedtime read."

Lynette Allen
*Creator: Her Invitation "Reminding women just how powerful & influential they really are"*
www.herinvitation.com

"So what can I say about Helen? From the minute I spoke to her I knew that she was someone that I wanted to work with. I love her energy, passion and enthusiasm for life, for the work she does and for the people she helps. Working with Helen for only a short time has already made me think about the way I approach my work in so many different ways. She has brilliant ideas and strategies that really work and she has an infectious personality. I always come away feeling motivated and inspired. She has transformed the way I work.

Jane Lowe
*Creator of Business Room 52*
www.br52.co.uk

"This book offers a practical approach to getting clarity and momentum around the right things to get your business going or growing. You will use it again and again!"

Ann Marie Mayling
*The Business SuperNanny*
www.annmariemayling.com

"Helen has created the ultimate 'plug and play' guide to landing clients in record time. Everything you need to know is right here. I highly recommend it to any coach, consultant or service based business owner."

Wendy Gannaway
*The Mindset Mentor*
www.onwards-and-upwards.com

"It's not enough to just have a good product or service; you have to know how to attract and keep clients. Helen's book does just that. An essential for any business if you want to succeed."

Deborah Durbin
*Journalist & Author*

———◆❦◆———

"I'm a big fan of Helen and her amazing work in helping entrepreneurs to get clients now. Packed full of practical tips and case studies as well as an effective and concise sales process to follow. This book is one of the most easy to use selling tools I have come across. This is a must read for all entrepreneurs who want to take their business to the next level and grow their sales."

Carole Bozkurt
*Blueprint Practice*
www.blueprintpractice.com

———◆❦◆———

"Helen Vandenberghe  has a way of making you feel good about taking action. She gets you fired up to get more clients, more deals and shows you exactly how to do it."

Jenny King
*Head of Sales*
Avanta

———◦◦◦———

"All professionals dream of a solid backlog of interesting and profitable clients but few understand how to achieve it. 'Get Clients Fast' fills this gap with the most comprehensive and actionable toolkit you'll ever need for building lifelong clients, at turbo speed."

Irma Bemudez"
*Author of The Six Pillars of Expertise*
www.irmabermudez.com

———◦◦◦———

"An inspiration and powerhouse of business and sales knowledge. Working with Helen has been a brilliant experience. Just the right balance of straight talking business advice, compassion when things get tough, and butt kicking when you're playing too small!"

Jane Simmonds
Natural Health Expert

———◄✦►———

"Helen Vandenberghe is an inspiring and very compassionate guide who has the ability to ignite 'the fire within' to be more, do more, have more, and give more. Her expertise and brilliant training system are a tremendous value that provide a framework and support system for success. She is an excellent role model. Knowing and working with Helen Vandenberghe is a real 'game changer'!

Teresa Blount
International Wellness Expert
teresablount.com

———◄✦►———

"Added an extra zero to my income! Powerful stuff— I wish I'd had this when I first got started over 10 years ago. I would have cut years off my success journey. Her brilliant system added an extra zero to my income in a year.

Caroline King
Voice Coach

# GET YOUR FREE RESOURCES HERE!

To download the free resources from this book,

Go to:

**www.GetClientsFastBook.Com**

———◦❖◦———

I wanted to make getting more clients as easy as possible for you, so we've put together a pack of valuable resources worth over $1,000 to help you implement each stage of the process.

These include downloadable and printable versions of checklists and worksheets along with a wealth of 'reader only' special bonus content.

Just go to our website **www.GetClientsFastBook.Com** and register to access all the bonus content including...

**GET CLIENTS FAST**

- ✓ Your Big Dream Worksheet

- ✓ Your Sales & Business Health Check (Value $197)

- ✓ Find Your Niche Checklist

- ✓ Social Media Checklist

- ✓ Your sales conversation planning sheet

- ✓ Annual Sales Planner

- ✓ Sales Call Record Sheet

- ✓ Your 30 Days Sales Plan(value $299)

- ✓ Get Clients Fast Audio Program (value $297)

- ✓ Business Revolution Summit Audio Program (value $199)

- ✓ Joint Venture Road Map (value $99)

**www.GetClientsFastBook.Com**

# THE LEGAL STUFF!

## Liability Disclaimer

By reading this book, you assume all risks associated with using the advice given below, with a full understanding that you, solely, are responsible for anything that may occur as a result of putting this information into action in any way, and regardless of your interpretation of the advice.

You further agree that the author and any company owned by her cannot be held responsible in any way for the success or failure of your business as a result of the information presented in this book. It is your responsibility to conduct your own due diligence regarding the safe and successful operation of your business, if you intend to apply any of our information in any way to your business operations.

## Terms of Use

You are given a non-transferable, "personal use" license to this book.

## Publishing Notes

## Credits

| | |
|---|---|
| Words: | Helen Vandenberghe |
| Cover Design: | Rebecca M. Durbin |
| Typesetting: | Jon J. Cardwell |
| Editing & Proof Reading: | Natalie Sullivan |
| | & Barbara D. Ayers |

# ACKNOWLEDGEMENTS

The strategies and ideas contained in this book are based on decades of experience. Like you, I'm sure, I have been a life-long learner and have been privileged to work with & learn from some of the absolute masters of sales, marketing & business growth (including Jeff Walker, Bernadette Doyle, Kat Loterzo, Lisa Sasevich, Christine Kane, Carly Hope, Melina Abbott & more).

I would like to thank all of my colleagues & mentors who have contributed so much to my learning and my success.

But my biggest thanks goes to my clients and community who have allowed me into their businesses and their lives, & have had the courage to stand up for a lifestyle they want.

Of course, none of it could happen without my home support team of Paul, Deb, Rich, Matt, Iris & of course Mum, & to all my friends and colleagues who have helped me shape my business and keep me inspired and energised.

Helen Vandenberghe

# PREFACE

From small beginnings....

I started my first business at the age of 14. I was visiting my local seaside town, hanging around the high street shops on a Saturday— like most teenagers - when I literally heard the bell toll!

Amongst the tinny pop music playing from the stores, I heard a clanging hand bell, & turned to see a lady dressed in a medieval costume shouting, "Come to Anna's market!"

I've always been a sucker for a fete, craft fair or frankly anything including bunting or balloons, and the potential of home-made cake, so I went across to the 'market' which was in fact just a load of tables in a church hall, and saw all of these lovely crafts being displayed.

There were paintings and hand-sewn goods, jams & wooden toys...and yes, even home-made cakes. I was in heaven.

Always eager to make some extra pocket money, I wondered if I could hire a stall and sell something. So I started chatting to the stall holders to find out more.

I'd previously done a project at school on the costs of setting up a retail store, and can remember thinking that I'd never be able to save up enough to pay for the rent, taxes, shop fittings, and staff, let alone stock. So this simple community market seemed like the ideal opportunity to me.

So I started my 'market research', with the vendors and soon discovered that a lot of them were not happy customers. Either— they didn't think there were enough visitors coming through the door— or when it was busy, the visitors were 'just looking' not spending, (I later learned that when you organise events you can never please everyone!).

Although there were exceptions, where particular products seems to sell like 'hot cakes', the majority didn't seem to be doing too well.

I was trying to figure out how they actually made any money. Maybe the table cost them 25 pounds to hire, and if they're only selling mugs at three pounds, they've got to sell quite a few just to break even.

Then it dawned on me that the only person guaranteed to make money was definitely the person who hired out the market stalls. I also could see that she had two sets of customers— one was the stall holders, who she needed to create the event, and the other was the visitors. I figured you probably needed to spend as much effort getting the right customers into the event as getting the right stall holders to attend.

**PREFACE**

So having had my traditional tea and cake, and bought a few items, I decided to set up my own market in my village. I collected all the business cards of the stall holders, and got the dates of the next 'Anna's markets' and planned to hold my own event in a different location on different dates so the stall holders had another opportunity to sell their products.

I started off just wanting to make some extra pocket money, but I soon learned that what I loved was creating events, bringing communities together and helping small businesses grow. That was my big 'why' —although I was unaware of it at the time.

I put a small lineage advert in the local paper, and soon people were calling to book a stall. I had to ask my Mum to stop saying "Helen's at school at the moment..." and start saying "Helen's out of the office right now, can I take your booking?", and soon I had my first event fully booked.

The first market went pretty well —it was 'the latest thing' in the village, and people were curious to see what was going on. At the second event, it rained and there weren't many people there. Suddenly I was the one dealing with grumpy stallholders, and had to get busy getting customers in and fast!

So, with the help of my CEO and my advisory board, i.e. my Mum and Dad we got in to action.

My Dad cycled around the village on his rickety old bicycle in the rain with a megaphone saying, "Come to Helen's market." And it worked! Dad stopped to chat to people on the way, and even took a detour in to the local pub, but after a refreshing pint, brought 50 people back with him! When they talk about getting your message out, I can't think of a better example of getting out and taking action. You can't sell from inside the church hall (or when hiding behind your computer!).

My Mum got some cakes from the corner shop and promised people that if they came to the market they could have a cupcake, or a fairy cake, as we used to call them.

I think that was my first experience of an 'ethical bribe'.

Years later one of my mentors talks about 'finding a hungry crowd' for your services but we literally did at the football and tennis club with hungry teenagers and bored Mums, we enticed them in.

So, I'd begun to understand how to get potential customers to an event, but I really wanted to figure out why some of the stall holders did well, and why some literally did nothing all day.

Over the two years that I ran the market, I learned more about sales behaviour, presentation, packaging and pricing than I ever did studying business studies in an academic environment, and started 'coaching' the stall holders on how to improve their sales.

Eventually it was time for me to move on to college, and so I handed over the market to a local community group, who ran it successfully for many years.

Since then, I've been fascinated with how businesses work. I couldn't help myself finding out why some entrepreneurs succeeded and others failed. I wanted to know exactly what they did and why? How they got those skills and how they could actually make a living out of it?

So that's how my career in business and sales began. It was much later, having built my own successful training and consultancy businesses that I discovered I could turn my fascination with sales and business strategy into a full time career helping companies to grow.

The path to your life's work is rarely straight— I haven't really had a career path— it's been more like 'crazy paving'.

Along the way I've hosted and spoken at entrepreneurship conferences with Sir Richard Branson, I've sold into, coached or trained in most of the FTSE 100. I've been the head sales trainer for Europe's fastest growing leisure company, CEO of an International learning organisation.

I've also taught salsa dance to an Arabian princess, dressed up as a chicken while leading 5 year olds in a theatre production, and been fired from a number of mind numbing cold calling jobs!

So if you think you don't have the right skills or background to grow your business and sell to clients— think again.

I was lucky to get some entrepreneurial lessons early on, but just like you, I've had my share of failures, fears and freak outs— and I'm sure there are more to come.

That small market was the start of some of my big dream of discovering and creating the work and the life I love.

My mission here is to help you do the same. Let's get started.

# TABLE OF CONTENTS

# GET INSPIRED

## Welcome to Get Clients Fast!

This book is designed to help practitioners, consultants, coaches, and trainers build and grow their business in a simple, systematic way taking the stress and struggle out of selling your services.

If you're tired of living 'client to client' and struggling to make the impact you want with your work, then you're in the right place.

Inside this book you'll find tips and techniques that can help you market and sell your services more effectively, and build the lifestyle you desire.  But, I warn you now— this may mean doing things radically differently to how you do them today.

You may need to change your thinking and almost certainly change parts of your business, and despite the title 'Get Clients *Fast*' , I'd be doing you a disservice if I didn't tell you there would be some ground work to be done.

**Top Tip - #1 Creative Strategy for your Brand**

The #1 creative strategy to creating a brand for your business that supports your six and seven figure goals is to create communication that expresses not where you are but for where you're going; that expresses your vision, your purpose and movement in the world.

As you are creating and expressing in your business, ask yourself "how can I, in this moment of expression, speak with the voice, words and power of the woman that is headed THERE vs. standing here?"

Honour where you are, most definitely, but realize that your ultimate vision, purpose and movement you stand for in the world is what you want to colour your communication with.

The double gift is that in doing so, it will help increase drive, confidence and keep you moving steadily towards your goals.

Michelle Ghilotti
*Couture Brand Creator and Success Coach*
www.michelleghilotti.com

Whether you're a new business owner or have been in the game for years, it's always useful to take stock and plan ahead for the next 6 - 12 months. So in addition to helping you create your 90 day marketing plan, we'll also be discovering your big dream (or mission), finding your ideal clients, and building the foundation of your business for the long term.

If you are someone who sells your expertise or your services through coaching, training or consultancy, it's likely that you're finding business tough going right now.

On paper, it's the ideal time to be an entrepreneur— it's never been easier to start, market, or manage a small business.

There are more low-cost and no-cost tools right at your fingertips than ever before. From social media and online videos, to hosted software programs like Infusionsoft and Clearbooks, to companies that allow you to build and launch a website in just a few hours, there's practically nothing you can't do right from your laptop.

Even better, the access to information, training, mentoring, coaching, and consulting— not to mention support from like-minded communities of small business owners— has never been more abundant.

So, we have the tools and the resources. We have the information. We have the ability to easily create visibility for ourselves. We have the like-minded communities overflowing with moral support.

---

### Top Tip - Manage the Angels and the Vampires

Energy Angels are tasks or those whom you surround yourself with that will give you energy. Energy Vampires will be people or tasks that drain you of energy. It can often be easy to get sucked in by the vampires and waste all of your energy on them when you should be focusing on the angels. Identify your angels and the clients will flow into your life with ease. When you do find them embrace them, they will bring you more clients and greater success.

Kelly Fryer
*Changing Mindsets, Transforming Lives*
www.chrysalis-consulting.co.uk

---

Why then, is it so tough?

Well, for one thing because despite all of the above, the success rate for small business owners continues to be abysmal. Figures published by HM Revenue and Customs that average income for self-employed entrepreneurs was just £9,800 (less than $15,000 dollars at time of going to press).

Isn't that shocking? And disappointing? And what about the rest of the business owners out there? How are the ones who do manage to make over £10,000 a year faring? Well, they're not doing much better.

Depending on which study you believe, anywhere from 80 to 90 percent of self-employed professionals earn under the six-figure level. And virtually every statistical report agrees that just one to two percent of solo business owners ever break the 7- figure ceiling.

**Top Tip - Achieve Peak Personal and Business Performance by Simply Rebuilding your Health**

It's no secret how stressful modern life has become. One in five Britons suffer from Anxiety or Depression and the number of anti-depressants prescribed in the UK has almost doubled in the last decade. On a daily basis we deal with highly demanding work, social and family life pressures. So much so that it can all feel a bit helpless at times. We have less time and as a result we turn to unhealthy habits such as fast food, soft drinks, coffee, smoking and alcohol. This in turn leads to ill health and under-performance, which increases the sense of pressure and the feeling of helplessness. How can you give your best to your business or to your family if your health is suffering? *Top Tip Continued...*

*...Top Tip Continued*

Invest in your health— mental, physical and spiritual - and the rest will follow.

Konstantinos Kapelas
*Rebuilds Health, Recharges Energy*
www.totalhealthnow.co.uk

And then there are the reasons you got into business for.

What about freedom, passion, wealth and impact?

If you're barely making ends meet in your business, then every decision that you make in your life, from what clothes you buy to which events you attend to which investments you make in your business to where and when (if ever) you take a holiday, are all driven first and foremost by money. In other words, you don't have freedom of choice when your choice is dictated by what you can and cannot afford (let alone if you are wondering, "Where in the world is my next client going to come from???").

Or maybe you're relying on your partner to pay the bills, but each month you find your confidence and credibility ebbing away as you suspect they think you've got an 'expensive hobby' not a business!

So while a lot of small business owners can choose when and where they work, what clients and projects they take on, and whether or not they want to hang out in their PJs all day— when it comes to bringing their 'vision boards' to life, and 'manifesting their 'financial goals' there's a huge gap that exists between their current reality and the life that they really want to live.

If this sounds familiar— let's explore this a little further here.

# Get Inspired

In this section we're going to look at what inspires you to do the work you do, and also what are some of your hopes, goals and dreams. We'll start with the big picture, and over the next few chapters, we'll be drilling down to specific details.

So let's think about your big dream as a business owner, and an entrepreneur. Why do you do what you do? Maybe it's freedom, contribution, or your big message... but none of it happens without the cash-flow to make it happen.

So let's start with the money, honey.

I really don't believe people just want to earn money. We don't try and make commerce just for lots of pictures of the Queen or a President on bits of paper.

We want to do something <u>with</u> that money. It has a meaning for us. So for some of you, it's about independence— being able to pay your way, provide for your family and make your own choices. For me, financial independence is a very big driver. Growing up I was blessed with an abundance of love, however, money was not so abundant in our household. I could see the stress that this caused my parents who worked so hard to provide for us, but never seemed to have quite enough for themselves.

For other people, it's about supporting our families, proving something to themselves, having luxury, looking after somebody we have cared for in our lives, or having time and freedom.

What are the things that you've been holding back on due to lack of money?

## Exercise

Jot down the things you'd be enjoying and investing in if your business was really rocking (maybe holidays, training, a new car, schooling for your kids?):

*continue your exercise here...*

As my business becomes more and more financially successful, I see myself enjoying...

## Create Your Own Vision Board

You might want to create your own 'vision board' to remind you of these hopes, goals and dreams.

A vision board is simply a visual representation of your goals. You can take a large piece of card, and a stack of old magazines, photos and pictures, and just cut out images that remind you of each item.

For example, if you'd love a particular car— try to find an image of the exact car (you could search on the internet then print it off, or order a brochure from the dealer). Alternatively, you could use images that inspire you, or that evoke the feeling you'll get when you achieve your goals.

I often cut out inspiring words and phrases too— for example 'Get Published' along with a picture of a stack of business books was on my vision board last year….. So I guess it worked for me!

For tips, ideas and examples of vision boards for business, visit our website www.GetClientsFastBook.com

Don't worry if the Vision Board 'thing' is not for you. Some people love lists or want to put their goals in a spread sheet. Do whatever works for you— but make sure you keep a record of your goals, hopes and dreams, and keep it somewhere visible, where you can see it every day.

## Let's Think About Impact

Most entrepreneurs I meet are not in business 'just' for the money. Many of us escaped a corporate job to be able to do more of the work we love and to make a real difference to the people we work with.

If more people or companies experienced working with you, what difference would this make? How would they benefit? What attitudes might shift?

In short, what is the impact you want to make in the world with your work?

## Case Study

One of my clients, Lynda, runs assertiveness workshops in schools and colleges. These give essential confidence and relationship skills to hundreds of young people each year. She's particularly passionate about those who have not been successful academically. Her work is changing the career and life prospects for many teenagers and young adults, who otherwise might be 'written off' by society. She loves to see them try new things and take on new challenges and while her business is making a considerable profit, she tells me her true 'payback' is helping shape an entire generation.

## Exercise

Spend a few minutes and jot down how the world be better if more people got access to your work now? (Fill in the box on the next page).

*continue your exercise here...*

## Now Go Deeper...

Now think about the **secondary** benefits that your work brings to your community.

When clients work with you they may, for example, come for help with their marketing. This is the primary benefit. But there are often 'follow on' benefits to the assignment.

In this example, when a client achieves better sales as a result of their new marketing strategy, this has a 'knock-on' effect in lots of other areas of their business and their life. These might include, improved visibility and reputation, better cash-flow, speaking opportunities, joint ventures, less stress at home - plus it may help build confidence of the business owner.

The impact is even greater with therapeutic and personal change services such as life coaching or career change or holistic or health services.

# Case Study

One of my clients owns a large dog training school. His primary concern is for the welfare of animals, and his work focuses on helping owners to build a successful relationship with their pet, and in turn have a well behaved dog.

However his customers have told him that other (secondary) benefits that come from his work include; increased confidence, better family relationships, less stress in their life, a sense of purpose and feeling more in control.

In the case of Lynda, working with young adults, some of the secondary benefits are; improved attendance and results for the school or college, higher quality course work, better relationships at home, less stress and friction for teachers and parents, unleashing hidden creativity and talents.

When clients work with you, what are the primary benefits they receive?

## Your Big Dream

If you are working with companies or individuals to create change, you probably have a big dream or mission that's driving your work.

Think about the long term change you would like to see in the world.

One of my clients aims to reach 1,000 women with her women's career development programme, with the aim of getting 20% more women in to board-level jobs in the next 3 years.

It's really important to know what your big dream is. What is the vision for your life, not just for your business? If you have growth goals of 60 percent or you want to get a 20 percent market share, there's a reason behind that. So what is that reason?

Knowing this can really help you achieve those goals.

If you've had those goals written down for a while and you haven't achieved them yet, then maybe you're just not in touch enough with the driving force behind them (or they're the wrong goals!).

To help you with this, I've created a worksheet for you to do, and some questions for you to sit down and work through. We will look at all the different areas of your life, including your finances, your relationships, your working schedule, your health, and your stress levels. The aim of this is to enable you to design your business to give you that lifestyle you want— rather than letting your business run your life.

If you've done it the other way around, as I certainly did with the first two businesses I started, it's very difficult when you've got a successful business, and even more so with a struggling one, to then try and create the life of your dreams when you've already got this monster that's out of control.

## Worksheet

Take some quiet time and to go through each question. Allow yourself time to think it through, and jot down your answers, then review it again in a few days.

So what's Your Big Dream?

What is your big dream for your business and your life? What would you like to create? Who would you like to serve? What's the big problem that you can solve?

Why is that important to you?

What is it that you can't help yourself doing? Where do you find yourself naturally 'interfering' and getting involved in things?

What does your intuition or higher power say about your gifts and what you are meant to be doing?

What do you want your business to give you? (Freedom? Security? A creative outlet?)

What would like your average working day, week and month to look like? How do you want to spend your time?

What goals do you have this year (in and outside of your business?)

How would achieving these affect the following areas?

Your working life

Your relationships

Your health

Your finances

Considering your answers above, what actions do you need to take?

## Check it Out Online!

For a downloadable version of this worksheet, plus tons of extra bonuses visit:

**www.GetClientsFastBook.com**

# GET REAL

In the last chapter, we looked at your big dreams, your big why and your goals for the future— so all the fluffy stuff!

Now don't get me wrong, I love all that stuff......but if you don't know exactly where your business is right now – what's working & what's not— those beautiful vision boards, and goals lists are just going to turn in to next month's recycling pile.

### Top Tip - What You Measure Expands

Tracking the numbers in your business may not be sexy but it is imperative to do this because what you measure you treasure. Money in particular loves being in relationship and you can only be in relationship if you are paying attention to it.

When working with clients the first thing I get them to commit to doing is to complete a money tracking sheet every day. On here they total up all the income that comes into their life that day. *Top Tip Continued...*

*...Top Tip Continued*

This might be revenue from sales to clients or it might be a rebate. It doesn't matter where the money comes from the important thing is to track it by noting it down. And if no money is coming in then put a zero. It's amazing how creative and focused you can get when you look at a sheet covered in zeros. It can really inspire you to find other ways to generate income.

As your business grows I would encourage you to start creating a business intelligence dashboard for your business that shows all the key metrics that impact your results. Examples of metrics that you might track include financial results, number of sales conversations, number of speaking gigs delivered, social media reach, number of people added to your list etc. The great news is that the changes in technology mean that it is easier than ever to get multiple sources of data aggregated and Joined Up into one simple dashboard.

Just like when driving a car you need to look at your dashboard to know where you are going, so it is the same in business. If you don't know your numbers you are effectively driving your business blind and this can be very dangerous.

*Top Tip Continued...*

*...Top Tip Continued*

So commit to tracking your numbers today, it will help give you clarity and show you where you need to focus your efforts to achieve your business goals.

Julia Felton
*Leader of the Joined Up Business Revolution, aligning leaders, teams and business systems to deliver greater sustainable productivity and profitability*
www.businesshorsepower.com

As someone who loves the big picture and hates the detail, I've learned the hard way how important getting clarity around your business is. Anyone else not know exactly what they made in the last month, or which marketing efforts are brought in the best returns? Yep, been there, done that.

This sort of thing will never be at the top of my priority list, and I'm guessing if you're a busy entrepreneur with a thousand ideas a day, then it might be the same for you. But let me reassure you— if I can do it, you absolutely can. And what's more, it is SO worth it.

So think of this as your business health check.

We will kick off by looking at what areas in your business and your working life are not performing effectively, and reviewing the ones that are, and what will have the biggest impact on your ability to attract clients.

---

### The Fastest Way to Double Your Conversion Rates

Do you have a product or service that truly delivers massive value, massive results or even massive impact? If not, this tip is not for you, skip ahead to the next tip. If so, consider a way to shift the risk from your prospects shoulders to your shoulders by using what I call "Results In Advance".

Developed with my work with my personal business coaches Jay Abraham and Rich Schefren, this is about completely eliminating the perceived risk of engaging or hiring you or your company.

Quite simple, yet profound in results. Offer for the prospect to pay you once they get results. And only when they get results.

Oh, and the best part is, you can (and should) charge much more. And they'll be happier that you did. And they'll refer more. Test this approach, you'll at least double your conversion rates.

*Double Your Conversion Rates Continued...*

---

> *...Double Your Conversion Rates Continued*
>
> For a video explaining this in detail visit:
>
> http://www.GetItTogether.com/results-in-advance-webinar
>
> Tom Matzen
> *International Best-Selling Author and Seminar*
> *Presenter*
> www.GetItTogether.com

In growing a small business, there's a whole lot of stuff that need to be monitored closely and should be reviewed regularly. But for most of us, more interesting stuff gets in the way.

If you want to have a better outcome in the next 6 months, start by reviewing the current six months first. I recommend you set aside an hour to complete a full review of the topics listed below. Be honest, and don't be too critical or beat yourself up. This is all learning and the information gleaned will be invaluable to your success going forward.

This 'Get Real' health check is in three sections, Financial, Operations & Marketing. You don't have to write a 'serious' business report. You can draw a mind map for each section, or discuss each of the areas with a coach or mentor and take notes for the answers.

Not all of the questions will be relevant to your situation, but don't skip the tricky stuff— it could be the key to taking your business to the next level.

# Financial

## 1. Review Your Income

What was your gross profit for the last 6 months?

What were your total expenses for the last 6 months?

What was your net profit for the last 6 months (i.e. total income minus expenses?

---

## Note from Helen...

Don't get discouraged by these numbers. They are not a measure of your worth. They are just numbers, and you can make them change as soon as you know where you're coming from.

There's space to write your answers below the questions, however we have also provided this as an editable document for you at www.GetClientsFastBook.com so you can complete it every 3 - 6 months to keep you on track.

## 2. Sales

Did you hit your sales targets? Write the reasons for your answer.

How many clients have you worked with in the last 6 months? Describe the products and services they bought.

On average, how long did they stay?

How did they describe their problem - what did they come to you for?

How well do your clients match up with your target client?

How much time per week do you spend selling (sales calls, meetings, contacting potential clients)? What does your answer tell you?

## 3. Service

How many clients had successful outcomes?

How many had unsuccessful outcomes, and why?

How many left before you thought they should have, and why?

Which clients are you most effective with?

Which do you enjoy the most?

## 4. Your Sales Funnel

Where did your clients come from? Advertising, networking, speaking, writing, referral partners etc... How did they find you?

What marketing efforts worked the best?

*Your Answer Continued...*

Who referred the most desirable clients? Who referred the least desirable?

How often do you contact your referral or joint venture partners?

## 5. Review Your Branding & Marketing Collateral

Is your business image consistent? (Business cards, website, logos, blog)

Is your website up to date?

Do any of your forms, brochures, or signs need to be updated?

Is it time to add colour and graphics?

## 6. Review Your Marketing Strategies

What strategies did you use in the last six months? (networking, speaking, writing, referral partners, advertising)

Which one(s) yielded the best results?

Which one(s) need improvement or more effort?

Which ones do you need to include next six months?

Are you reviewing costs frequently?

Do you keep a close enough eye on your direct costs, your overhead and your assets?

Are there different ways of doing things or new materials you could use that would lower your costs?

Can you negotiate better deals with your suppliers?

## 7. Review Your Products and/or Services

How effectively are you matching your goods and services to your customers' needs? If you're not quite sure what those needs are, you could carry out further market or customer analysis.

Which of your products and services are succeeding?

Which aren't performing as planned? Decide which products and services offer both a high percentage of sales and high profit margins.

Are there any poorly-performing products or services you should drop?

What's really behind the problems of a product or service?

Consider areas such as pricing, marketing, sales and after-sales service, design, packaging and systems during your review.

Look for 'quick wins' that give you the breathing space to make more fundamental improvements.

## 8. Review Environment and Competitors

Did any major competitors enter your market?

*Your Answer Continued...*

Any relevant news stories or controversy this six months?

Has your neighbourhood changed?

Have circumstances made your office more or less visible/accessible?

Are other businesses or competitors moving into or out of the market?

How do your competitors compare with your products or service offerings?

# Operations

## 1. Client Management

Are your procedures defined & consistently followed for...

Client intake?

Communications?

Service reviews?

Request for referrals?

Follow up?

## 2. Procedures

Can office procedures be streamlined, computerized or contracted out for better productivity?

What systems do you have in place?  What do you need to redefine or set up?

## 3. Review Your Liability

Lease agreements, partnerships and other documents that impact your business.

Is your liability insurance coverage adequate and current?

Is this the six months to incorporate?

Consult professionals about making appropriate changes, and meet with your financial advisor and accountant for a six months-end review and tax planning.

## 4. Review Your Premise

What are the advantages and disadvantages of your current location?

Do you have room to grow, or the flexibility to cut back if necessary?

If you move premises, what will be the cost? Will there be long-term cost savings and improvements in efficiency?

*Your Answer Continued...*

Does your office space need an upgrade?

## 5. Information Technology

What information management and other IT systems do you have in place?

Will these systems suffice for any proposed expansion?

Do they assist in making a difference to the quality of the products or services your business provides? If they don't, can you change them to make sure they do?

Do you make the best use of technology such as wireless networking and mobile telephony, to allow for more flexibility?

## 6. People and Skills

Do you have the right people to achieve your objectives?

Do they know what is expected of them?

Do you do performance reviews?

Do you have a training and development plan?

Do you pay as well as the competition?

Do you suffer from high staff turnover?

Are employees/outsourced staff motivated and satisfied?

Do you have the right team in place for growth?

Does your staff need new or improved skills? Does it need to be retrained?

Do you have or need contractors or outsourced help like Virtual Assistants, Graphic Designers, SEO specialists, Web Designers?

## 7. Professional Development

Do you have the skills available that you need in areas such as human resources, sales, and IT?

What professional skills development do you need to further enhance your quality service?

Is it time to hire a mentor, consultant, or coach to get better results?

## 8.Your Professional Status

What associations do you belong to?

Have you participated or attended often enough?

Should you volunteer for a committee or executive position?

What benefits or business did you get from your membership —is it time to leave?

What associations or professional organizations could you join? Consider which ones your target prospects or potential referral partner attend.

**So what have you learned?**

Firstly– a HUGE congratulations for completing this Business Health Check.

Or did you skip over a few sections?

 OK, so we're all human– but I urge you to go get a huge mug of hot chocolate, coffee or a pot of tea, and hunker down and DO THE WORK!!

So I'm going to assume you're a kick-ass entrepreneur who is taking their business seriously, and you've got on and done it!

You probably now know more about your business than most FTSE100 Executives do about theirs!

So what have you learned?

Take a moment and focus on which one task you want to address in each section.

Go to **www.GetClientsFastBook.com** and download your *Business Health Check Strategy Plan*, where you can log your goals and track your progress.

Woo hoo! You're on your way!

Now let's get you 'niched'!

# GET NICHED

## Understanding Your Ideal Clients

In the last chapter you examined your business with a fine tooth comb even. Now you need to do the same for your ideal client base. I cannot stress how important it is for you to have a strong niche, and to market specifically to it.

**Success Story:**
**LinkedIn Works Like Client Attraction Magic**

A few months ago a new client shared a very difficult piece of information with me— he needed my services, but couldn't afford to pay me because his business was almost bankrupt. Please would I consider a credit card payment? I was his last resort. This was it. His final business stake was to see if LinkedIn could change his business fate and no pressure for me (not much!). But it needed to happen fast! *Success Story Continued...*

*...Success Story Continued*

I set to work rewriting his personal LinkedIn profile. That's right. I didn't create a business page. Or a group. I rewrote his personal profile page.

Actually, we should rewind...

The first thing I did was to ask questions and listen, listen, listen, listen to every single piece of career history there was. From leaving education to the present day. I took pages (and pages) of notes. Asked for copies of 'About' pages. Old CVs. I asked about clients, success stories, qualifications and why each career choice had been made and what was really good about it.

From there I was able to craft (and it really is a craft—kind of like great art) a profile that told a story. His story. His compelling, credible, book-him-in-a-heartbeat story.

I closed my eyes, held my breath... and sent the draft of the new profile over for review... and once we'd agreed it, I uploaded it.

Pan forward three days. 72 tiny hours. For a business that had been struggling for a long time....

*Success Story Continued...*

*...Success Story Continued*

72 miniscule hours after I hit 'save' on that new LinkedIn profile, he had 3 new clients!!! That's right, not one enquiry. Three new clients. Worth thousands of pounds. Paying my fees. His expenses. And giving the business some much needed cash flow and profit.

Many people tell me they 'don't get' LinkedIn. That as it may be, it is reportedly 277% more effective for lead generation than Facebook and Twitter. Can you afford to not even try?

Julie Holmwood
*LinkedIn Whisperer*
www.julieholmwood.com

If you sell lots of different services to lots of different people try to focus on just one area for now, and do it well.

Let's look at defining your ideal client:

Who are they?

Where can you find them?

What problem(s) do they have that you can address?

In this section, we really need to get into the mind-set of the ideal customers, learn to speak their language, and see things from their point of view. So what do we mean by getting niched? Quite literally it means who are you aiming your products or service at?

The most disheartening thing I hear back is, "Everyone."

Well, I sell massage. So anyone could benefit from that. I sell assertiveness training or confidence training and anyone could do that. Now you're absolutely right, almost anyone could use those services. But trying to sell to anyone or everyone indiscriminately is extremely difficult, and you just don't have the market— and probably don't have the income —to be a global brand. The sorts of people that sell to everyone are your massive multimedia brands, but even they target a very specific sector of the huge market.

If you look at Coca-Cola, it has a massive appeal. You might say, "Well, anyone might drink it." But they know that really their primary market is teenagers, specifically between the ages of 13 and 17, because if you can attract someone's drinking habits at that early age, then they're likely to continue that well into adulthood. Even these massive global brands who have products that anyone could use have a niche. I'm sure you do see 90-year-olds swigging back the Coca-Cola as well, but actually that's not their ideal market.

So we need to think about who really is the ideal client for your product or service. You want a very narrow but deep niche. For example, as a training organisation you might be able to focus on customer service training, which you could sell to almost any company in the country. But if you become a specialist in the area that you've delivered the most service in, maybe customer service training for hotels, it suddenly becomes a whole lot easier to find potential customers. It becomes easier to tailor your materials so it speaks directly to their needs. After all, someone who's worried about customer service in a hotel is not going to have the same concerns as somebody who is dealing with customer service in a garage.

There will be some commonalities, but there will be very big differences about the way they treat their own clients, about the language they use, and about the challenges that they face. Even the way they recruit people, and the way they train people will all be done differently.

## A Fame Name® Nails Your Niche
## (& Sells You in 20 Seconds)

I love Fame Names® —but then I would say that as I am famous for them! A Fame Name® is a personal headline that instantly tells us who you are, what you do and who you do it for. When you've worked out your niche it gives you a spotlight as 'The' person who does what you do.

Fame Names® work because of how we remember people. We're wired to remember what someone does much more than we're wired to remember a name. Being remembered means you get referred, and that means new clients.

Here's a great example of a Fame Name® in action. Jennifer is The Flow Writer— she helps people to flow their words into brilliant writing (usually a book)....

*Nailing Your Niche Continued...*

*...Nailing Your Niche Continued*

....She works with speakers, experts and all manner of smart people who are stumped when it comes to writing their stories.

Jennifer was at an event recently for a 'big name' speaker. The room was packed. As part of the day the audience formed groups to take part in exercises. With just seconds each they introduced themselves. When you have a Fame Name® it sticks in people's heads, telling them exactly what you do and for whom. So when Jennifer said, "I'm the Flow Writer, and I help brilliant people write their book in their voice," her group was super clear on what she does. And it stuck.

Fast forward a few weeks and one of the group from that day is asked by a friend 'Do you know anyone who can help me write my book?' Of course the answer was yes— the lady knew Jennifer. She knows she is The Flow Writer, so a quick Google and the friend gets help. Bear in mind the event was in London, and this friend is in the US. It only took 20 seconds for Jennifer to stick in someone's head, get filed away, move countries and show up when asked for.

*Nailing Your Niche Continued...*

*...Nailing Your Niche Continued*

It's not enough to know your niche, you want to be the 'name' in it too.

Lucy Whittington
*Talent Manager and Author of*
*FindYourThingBook.com*
www.beingabusinesscelebrity.com
*and* www.findyourthingbook.com

I'd like you to jot down right now as many potential clients and potential niches you could serve with one core product, program or service.

I know that you may have lots of different services, but let's get one nailed and selling really effectively, and then you can use that and model these techniques for other areas of your business.

Let's pick one. I've already mentioned you needing a narrow and deep niche so let's take a second to expand on that: you want something that's very specific, but that has plenty of people. So you probably don't want something that is so rare and so extreme that it's impossible to find customers within your locality, or easily on the internet. You want a group of people who have that need within a particular sector.

For example, let's say that you are a massage therapist or a physiotherapist. Then you might choose to focus on people who are running marathons, and the benefits, opportunities, and issues that they have. If I'm a runner and I'm looking for a physiotherapist, I'm on your website and I see pictures and case studies of how you've helped runners improve their personal best time, and I see examples, quotes and testimonials from people who are like me and they are beginner runners, then over the choice of all those other competitors, I'm probably more likely to choose you. Are there enough runners in your country? Probably yes, if you're in a Westernised country. Then yes, it's an extremely popular sport or pastime.

That's what I mean by a narrow but deep niche. We've narrowed our target market to a specific group of people (runners) and we know that there are plenty of people in that group (the well is deep!).

Let's spend some time thinking on that and just jot down your thoughts in the book here, or in the materials that are on the website.

Okay, so having thought about a niche, let's get into the mind-set of the people in it. We call these people your ideal clients or your avatars.  Who is your ideal client within your niche? Going back to our earlier example, you might say runners. But if you think, well ideally, I want someone training for their first marathon, you could do some research and find out what is the average age of the people who start training for a marathon.

I can tell you the average age of runners that start training is 31, particularly for men. They're usually slightly later (in their 40's) for women.  But it's quite easy to just do some research on Google about what the average of certain things are.  For example, the average age of people starting to learn to cook, or take driving lessons etc.

Do some research around your niche and create a profile of your ideal customer. So what sort of place do they live in? What do they do? What are their concerns and worries within the realm of your service?

So again, let's stay with the running example.

Common issues are not having a training plan; getting injuries early to midway through their training; learning how to improve their time once they get start getting good; not knowing what to eat; and worrying about how much rest they should have. All of these thoughts and feelings and fears are pretty common to first time marathon runners— your ideal client. So that's the sort of the level of detail you need to start with, and then go much deeper around what it is that they really need, and what keeps them awake at night. What do they worry about?

---

**Top Tip - Create an extraordinary personal brand**

The online market place is busy and getting busier. After all, having your own business is an ideal tool for you to create the level of choice and freedom in your life. So how do you stand out from others who offer a service similar to yours? Build an extraordinary personal brand. Be clear and visible in who you are, what you stand for. Share your core brand stories in all you do. You'll become the go-to person for a certain type of client and others will be able to refer you more easily.

Caroline Cain
*The Freedom Seeker's Business Mentor*
www.carolinecain.com

---

Jot down and spend some time thinking about your ideal clients, and if you know somebody, if you've worked with somebody, or you may be currently working with somebody, go and interview them. Find out, and listen to their language.

People don't typically say, "I need a homeopathic massage to remove the viscous tissue in my torn ligament."

What they go with is, "I want to get rid of my knee pain." That's what they're likely saying or "I wish I could get upstairs again." That's the language you want. So you can use that throughout all of your sales conversations and your marketing material.

We really need to get into the mind-set of your ideal customers and speak their language. You will find at the end of this chapter a whole list of questions that will get you thinking about what do they think, what do they feel, what is their biggest problem and what is the language they use? What are the actual words they say?

Then you can think about all the opportunities to help them.

## Worksheet

## Find Your Niche

Do you know who you want to help?

The answer here should not be, "I can help everyone." If you want to market online with that lack of clarity you'll drown. Offline won't be much better unless you're a real networking dynamo and can change hats faster than a stand-up comedian.

Do these 'perfect clients' have the ability to pay what you want to charge?

A good example of this is if you want to work as a career coach, and work with women to help them get back into the job market.

How will they pay you?

_____

_____

_____

They either need to have the income to do so or you can align yourself with an organization that has funding to pay you. Otherwise you'll be a frustrated, broke coach or service provider!

Can you reach your perfect clients in large numbers?

_____

_____

_____

You will need to get your solution in front of a lot of ideal clients for some of them to be in the right place to enroll with you today. You need to know where to find them online and preferably offline too.

Do you know which keywords your perfect clients are tapping into Google to seek out the solution you offer?

_____

_____

_____

_____

_____

_____

_____

If not, you're going to have a hard time being found online without being glued to social media all day. Why not set up your online platform to generate highly targeted niche leads. (It's not as hard as it sounds.)

Who are your direct competitors?

_____

_____

_____

_____

---

---

---

Study their style and how they deliver their coaching and programmes. If you don't bother with this, how can you find your way to stand out? Yes, being your authentic self is a great start, but you also need to be able to communicate your value in practical terms.

What is their pain? What is their biggest and most pressing issue? (You can make a list and brainstorm if you have to, but find ONE that is the most important.)

---

---

---

---

---

---

---

What is the most important promise they really want to hear? (You can make a list and brainstorm if you have to, but find ONE that is the most important.)

_____

_____

_____

_____

What other areas in life are affected by this pain? What specific instances (time, form, place, event, result)?

_____

_____

_____

_____

_____

_____

_____

**GET REAL**

How long has it been going on?

_____

How much time is wasted from the solving the problems?

_____

_____

Why is it logical that they cannot solve it themselves? (We are looking for face-savers)

_____

_____

_____

_____

_____

_____

_____

Why is it not their fault that they have this pain? How did life circumstance make it so they had no choice but to have this pain/problem? What reasons can we find that your prospects and reasons for having this pain are unique to them vs. others?

_____

_____

_____

_____

What would life be like without the pain? Show the reverse of the things identified above.

_____

_____

_____

_____

_____

_____

# GET PACKAGED

Now it's time to discover how to package your services for profit!

Imagine that for every sale you made, for every sales conversation you had, you could make five times— or even ten times— the return for the same effort. Well, that's what packaging your programs, products, and services does, because frankly, it takes just as much effort to sell a single session, or a single product as it does an entire suite of products, a program, or a service.

What I want to recommend you to do, is to start bundling up your product or your services into compelling packages and building irresistible offers that make people just want to purchase them straight away, and that gives you huge value and builds a much longer relationship with that client.

Here's an example. If you're say, a nutrition coach, and you currently sell individual sessions by the hour, I think the first step for you is to sell them in groups. So you might sell six sessions, but typically, what people do then is they sell six sessions for the price of five. So they're now working harder for less money, but this does mean that you don't have to sell those individual sessions each time, so there is some benefit there. It does mean that you're actually getting a little money for the work you're doing.

What I would look at is who the premium buyers in your market are because every market has some. There are people who would just pay money for getting an issue fixed or creating an opportunity. So who are the premium buyers and what do they want?

What could you put together that would combine the services you already offer, plus something that could be really valuable for them, but would take little cost or time to deliver?

Here's an example. Go back to our nutrition coach. Lots of people want a nutrition plan, but actually there's often some lifestyle issues there as well, and there are often some health issues too. They might need supplements, or they might not be that great at cooking. It can be a real issue for people when they're trying to change their diet— and actually if they're not that confident in the kitchen, they're never really going to get around to changing those issues, to trying out those new recipes.

There's a whole range of other things there that are common issues for people who might come to a nutritionist that could be offered to them as a complete package. Rather than it being a one to one or a one-hour nutrition session, it's a weight loss six-month programme, or it's a 're-energise your life' three-month boot camp, or something like that. You would have to choose a language that is appropriate to your market.

The idea is that you select the items that you could add in that would add massive value. The items that would serve my clients and give them a much better service stop me having to go back to reselling to them, get them working with me longer, and also get great results for them.

### Top Tip - Choose Your Clients!

Having run my business for almost 11 years I've learnt some very powerful lessons about attracting clients. Perhaps the main one is - really take time working out exactly who your ideal client is.

In the early days I was so focused on getting as much paid business as I could that my strategy was to say yes to virtually anything and anyone. This meant that my clients were a mixture of some who were a good 'fit' for me and some who definitely were not.

Although I believe flexibility in approach is important, I was finding that I was having to adopt many different personas in order fit with them. *Top Tip Continued...*

*...Top Tip Continued*

....Whilst it brought in quite a lot of business it came with quite a lot of stress too and looking back I think I lost a lot of me as I was trying to be everything to everyone. I knew I couldn't continue working for clients and doing work that didn't truly fit me.

In the last couple of years I have taken a really good look at who my ideal client is by literally drawing up a profile (and yes I do mean draw!) of who they are, what they stand for, their values, beliefs and the specific type of work that I would be involved in with them. Drilling down and 'drawing' into that level of detail made my ideal client (and ideal work) so much more real.

By putting all my faith, focus and belief that these are clients who I deserve and who deserve me has given me the heightened level of awareness and inspired ideas to connect with them. In some ways it's been a courageous decision because it's meant that I cherry pick the work I truly want and I've had to accept that I've got less business than I once had...in the short term.

What I'm noticing now is that by making a definite decision to close some ill-fitting doors, other better fitting doors are opening! *Top Tip Continued...*

In the corporate world, we train and we often sell in individual courses, and I always think this is a huge mistake. Somebody phones up and sells a training course for time management, yet often when you get in to facilitate that course, you realise there are much bigger challenges. This isn't about to-do lists, this is probably about communication. This is probably about managing the challenges between different departments, or even looking at the system.

As part of that time management programme, you might include some pre-work that could be done online. That would give you analysis. You could host a conference call that would get the work started before you even attended.

You could do some post-evaluations that could feed back into their survey. You could provide one-on-one coaching to people so that they actually implement what they've learned. So that would be an entire programme that would sell for much more and be much more effective than a single day or two-day training course.

At the back of this chapter and in our online content you'll find some tools to show you how can you design products and programmes and bundle up your goods together.

Is it time for you to have your own high ticket coaching package? If you prefer to work with clients at a deep level, but want to move on from classic one-to-one coaching or consulting into long term programmes, then you're ready to create a bundled programme your clients will love!

Go for high quality, high impact time with your clients. But be sure to play to your strengths, while also considering what people in your market really want. Some markets will be too busy for individual calls and prefer live events at an exciting destination where they can tack on vacation time. Some markets will want more "hand holding", so you'll want to load on opportunities for both group and private support.

What is the ONE key problem your package or programme will solve?

What is your system or process (break down how you achieve your result into 5 - 8 steps?)

Over what time period will you offer this service?

# Pre-start Review Tools

- Analysis or research

- Deep dive intensive 1:1 session

- Coaching

- Mentoring

- Educational teleseminars

- Webinars

- Live events

- Away day

- Software

- Books

- Video/Makeover/Photos

- Recourses

- Done for you services

- Community membership

- Networking opportunities

## Bonuses

What valuable extra resources could you include?

- Educational modules

- Exercises

**GET PACKAGED**

- Templates

- Checklists

- mp3s/ CDs

- Books/eBooks

Scribble your ideas down here:

As with all offers, design your package to include all or a subset of the following benefits:

**Educate**. Fill the holes in your market's knowledge.

**Correct**. Help them stop making the same mistakes and create better habits.

**Simplify**. Show them how to do something in a step-by-step format.

**Shift**. Bust myths, breakthrough to more powerful mindsets, open their eyes to a better way.

**Inspire**. Motivate them to take action, stay the course, and keep the faith.

Added to these is the wonderful value of community and connection.

# GET VISIBLE

This chapter is all about marketing yourself, since that's actually going to help you get leads. It could also be called "How to Be Seen as an Expert in Your Field and Have Clients Calling You!"

You need to fill your funnel and get lots of leads, so they can lead you into potential sales conversations.

Let's look at some of the most accessible ways of doing that and getting out there. Let's start with social media in this section.

We're going to be looking at the ways that social media could help you attract clients and build your list.

First of all, you can waste a huge amount of time on social media. If you're not doing it strategically, you almost certainly will.

We need to start with the end in mind. What is it that you want people to do, when they encounter you on any form of niche? You need to have a very clear sales funnel and so this means thinking right.

Somebody hears about me in one way or another, and what I want is for them to download something. I would like their email and ideally their phone number. But certainly their email address, so that I can then engage them in an email conversation and then later invite them to a real conversation.

For me, the purpose of any marketing I do is that people engage with me and they join my list. For any social media post, if you just put "Join my Free Newsletter," it's not going to work. Nobody has the time. Nobody is interested and people are really getting too many emails. They're worried about spam.

You need to make sure that you give them something really valuable in exchange for their email address, and also give the option to completely unsubscribe after they've received your valuable free gift.

Let's talk about a valuable free gift to start with. You need to create some reason that somebody on social media— or any other media— would engage, and would give you their details.

Let's say we've thought about the ideal niche and we now know what the problems of the ideal audience is. Let's say you're a trainer and you're selling time management training, and often that's to an organisation. What would be really useful to somebody purchasing that?

First of all, we need to know who the customer is. Now, is the customer the person who actually attends the course? Their manager? Or is it the person in HR or business strategy that decides that we need more time management training? You need to decide that first because I would create a different, valuable free offer or report for each of those people.

Let's say that it is your busy front line manager who wants his team to perform more effectively. In that case I might create some kind of free gift, a report or an easy tool, maybe a time tracking tool, or something like "Ten Tips to Help Your Team Be More Productive". Something that's easy to create, easy to download, or to send on, and also that might get shared around. Of course your details are going to be on it and you actually want people to share it.

That's the beginning with the end in mind, your strategies for all of these methods.

Then what I want you to do is to create your free offer, and then create relevant posts about it on social media. The way I work is this: I start with creating a free report, which is my "Ten Ways to Help My Team Be More Productive."

Then, from that free report, I will just pull off some of the keywords or the key phrases. So I might have tip number one, 'What you don't measure, you can't manage,' or something like that.

What I might do next is use a comment from a social media

post which will then drive people to a webpage, to then get them to download the report, which makes them exchange their email.

There's a whole process there, based on the things that my potential clients could be interested in. What are the tips? How can I use social media to engage people rather than just blast them?

### Make Sure You're on LinkedIn - Properly

People use LinkedIn for search… and to do due diligence. If they can't find you, they may dismiss you altogether. Equally, if what they find doesn't tick the 'credibility box', you're out of the running before you can say 'rewriting my LinkedIn profile is next on my To Do list'. Think about what you would tell your dream prospect about your career-to-date if you were face-to-face. THAT is what your LinkedIn profile needs to say!

Julie Holmwood
*LinkedIn Whisperer*
www.julieholmwood.com

On our bonus content online for this book at **www.GetClientsFastBook.com**, you can find social media planning templates, which will give you the ideas of what content you should put where. Let's start with that. Just getting your name out there with something really useful would help.

Number two is connecting with past colleagues, employers, and employees through LinkedIn. You're much more likely to sell to people or to someone who you know has met you before. Likewise, people love to recommend great resources.

If you've done a great job for somebody in the past, they may not be your ideal client right now, but they might know someone who is. Those people are great to get back in touch with, because they can be your best evangelists.

Your task for this week is to track down people that you've worked with and just put them in to LinkedIn. Get an account if you haven't already and search places you've worked, people you've connected with in the past and start connecting with them on LinkedIn. Just say hi and see if you can arrange a time for coffee if you live nearby or a phone chat and just catch up with them. I'll talk about what you should say during these conversations in our bonus material.

Now let's look at writing articles and blogs, etc. You've probably got a lot of knowledge in your head about your specialist subject but writing can be tough for some people— if you're one of them you can just talk into your computer or into a conference call and record it, then have someone else transcribe that for you!

Writing articles and blogs can be a fantastic way of connecting with people around the world. This isn't about a sales article. This is about showing some expertise, and then of course everything that you publish should have a link to your funnel whether it's your website or a phone number where people can contact you.

We're going to write at least four blogs or four articles a month. Publishing on your own blog is not super effective until you've got a great following, but it can be very good to write on other people's blogs. Again, in our resources page, you will find some tips on how you can get blogs published on other people's sites.

## Success Story - Get Yourself Noticed

I recently worked with a client who wants to write a book to boost her business. Now, we both agreed that this is one of the most impactful tasks to set yourself up as a business owner. It's a great way to build your expert status, get known and attract potential clients. When your book hits number one on Amazon, then people really do sit up and take notice! But, of course, it takes time to plan, write, promote and launch your book. *Success Story Continued...*

*...Success Story Continued*

Publishing something which conveys your message to the world can't be done in a weekend but is quite comfortably done in six months if you give it your focus and commitment. But my client, Chris, wanted to get immediate results to make her more visible as well as help with the eventual writing project. So I got her working on article writing as a start. Inevitably Chris made the comment I hear often: "I don't know what to write about!" so we brainstormed around what she does and how she helps her current clients, and together came up with a list of key issues she could write about. That was a great start for her! She was delighted to have a list of 12 topics that she could take out to potential clients to help them from where they are now, but also to show how powerful her work is and how they may benefit from knowing more. Let's not forget that the objective is not just to provide solutions today but to quickly attract new clients to work with us further down the line! Articles don't need to be long— 500 or 600 words is fine (that's about twice length of this contribution if you're wondering!) and will provide you with content you can post on article submission sites on the internet and on your blog or in your newsletter. Use them to drive traffic to your website so people can find out more about you. *Success Story Continued...*

*Success Story Continued...*

And articles, as Chris who is now in my book writers mastermind group found, can form the skeleton plan of your book and inspire you to get round to writing it!

Kate Cobb
*The Book Writers Mentor*
www.bookwritersacademy.com

Here's a really simple thing you can do to get visibility and start establishing your new niche. Just put a footnote on your email signature, inviting people into a discovery call, a conversation, or a free consultation. For example, "If you would like to learn more about this, click here for the opportunity for a 15-minute free discovery call," something like that.

You will be amazed by the results! About 17 percent of my new clients come from this method alone. So that's people who receive an email from me and have clicked through and booked discovery sessions— or you might call it a sales conversation, a strategy session, or a free consultation. What that means is it's a sales call with a structure.

So let's say you're a natural health coach and actually you do body work. Then you're not going to book people in for a free appointment where they do work with you. But most people want to phone up and see if they like the sound of somebody before they work with them. It could be a 15-minute health check. It could be a phone consultation which gives you the opportunity to sell them into a programme.

So you could send emails to all the contacts that you have. This covers anyone within your professional and personal network. Of course, be mindful that they do need to be people that you genuinely know and have had contact with in the past. You could email them with a special invitation to a call.

Maybe you could run a conference call. You could just invite people into a discovery session. This could go along the lines of, "I'm just launching or re-launching my new 'XYZ' service. I've been very fortunate to work with people like this and they've been getting these results. If you think this might be something that you would love to learn some tips about, and how to achieve these results in your business, then why not book in for a discovery session?" Again, a massively effective tactic.

One of the best ways of getting visibility is through attending and speaking at networking groups. In the next chapter, we're going to talk you through giving a presentation at a networking group, and how you can make that super effective for sales, so that you don't spend all your time eating poor quality sausage rolls and being bombarded by accountants! We attend networking meetings because everyone needs an accountant. They're great for them but for many of us, it means being sold at, rather than having the opportunity to sell. But no more!

If you're attending networking groups, first of all, you want to hang out with your clients, not with your peers, for sales. Obviously it's great to connect and speak with people who are in the same business as you, for support and encouragement.

When you've got selling on your mind, then you really want to make sure that you are connecting with your ideal clients. So if you are somebody who sells psychometric tests to mid-level managers, you want to be talking to mid-level managers and going to their events, rather than to meet other people who are psychotherapists or who run psychometric tests.

Choose your networking groups carefully. You want to be thinking about your final objective. This isn't about hounding people so that they work with you. It's about giving people the opportunity to connect with you on a free strategy session, or that you have a valuable free gift for them.

All of those can be great tactics to start with. Then the other thing that you might want to do in networking groups is actually get the opportunity to 'guest speak'. You definitely want to speak to the host, give them as much support, offer to help, and when it's appropriate, offer to speak.

Those are some ideas on how you can get visible.

# Prepare

- Create a user-friendly website where customers can easily find your services and contact information.

- Set concrete goals for what you want to achieve by being on social networks. Do you want to promote a product, drive more people to your website, get feedback or create brand awareness?

# Learn

- Find out your clients' favourite social media plat-forms. Looking for a new customer demographic? Research which social media networks they are most likely to join.

- Pick one or two social media channels. Learn how they work, how to create an account, post content, and add visuals and videos.

- Find out what people are looking for or discussing, and look for trends.

- Monitor how other businesses are engaging their customers.

- Research your competitors' social media activities to see what is working best for them.

- Join the conversation yourself to see how it works.

## Analyse

- Calculate how much time, effort and money you will need to write engaging content and maintain your presence on social media.

- Figure out how often you should post and respond and the best time of day to reach your customers. Create a calendar to make sure that you post regularly.

- Build trust by providing value-added information and not simply promotional advertising. Ask yourself, would you follow an account that posted the same amount of self-promotional messages?

- Find an analytics tool to help you monitor and measure your progress in achieving your goals.

## Network

- Participate actively in the conversation to help you gain the trust of your network.

- Have a protocol for dealing with positive and negative feedback.

- Listen to your virtual community and be prepared to make improvements based on its suggestions.

It takes time to create a plan, but once it's completed you'll be ready to make the jump into social media and establish a new way of communicating and networking with your customers.

### Top Tip - Why Your Business Needs a Book

Getting known for what you do has become increasingly difficult, as there are likely to be many people selling something similar to you. To be successful, you have to find what makes you different, enabling you to stand out.

The advice by many is to niche. It can feel counterintuitive, but as I found out last year, the deeper and narrower you go, the easier it can be to grow your business.

Last year I was approached by coaches who I've known for a while to help them with their books. As a published author myself (with three books under my belt and another on the way), I realised that I had found my point of difference. *Top Tip Continued...*

*...Top Tip Continued*

....It is often the thing you find easy that other people need to know about.

Writing a book isn't for the fainthearted, but you'll find that it will enable you to grow your business. Importantly it will help you to get clear on what it is that you actually do, who you love to work with, and where you are an expert. When you know who your clients are and where they need help, you can package up your expertise into a system or process that they want.

Your book is the hook that gets you noticed. It is a brilliant marketing tool if you want to open new doors or get more opportunities for speaking, PR or simply to reach more people. Prospective clients who have already invested in your knowledge in your book are likely to be your best advocates, and keen to work with you on a deeper level. Also, a book also allows people to find out more about you before they say yes, enabling you to win new business without pushy sales tactics.

That's why I've written and published my latest book 'Your Book is the Hook', as this shows you how it's done.

*Top Tip Continued...*

*...Top Tip Continued*

I also now help many of my clients to write their own book that is the hook to grow their business.

Karen Williams
*Business and Book Mentor*
www.selfdiscoverycoaching.co.uk

# GET TALKING

This section is all about structuring effective sales conversations and doing your research. Most people get quite scared about feeling too 'salesy' or pushy on a sales call or a conversation with potential clients. But if you really believe in your product or service, if you really believe that it can help the client, then think of it as a conversation to see if you're a match— no pressure and no hard sell.

The first thing is around getting your mind-set right. One of the ways I've been able to sell very high end programmes successfully is by completely falling in love with the programme to create whatever I'm selling. Whether it's a product, a service or a programme, really understand what the benefits are and what it can do for the potential client. Know that regardless of whether they're a fit or not, if you feel that your product or service isn't, then there's some work to do there.

If you're working for yourself, then you have complete control over that. If you're working as an affiliate to somebody else, then you can liaise with them. Maybe you need to find other products and services to sell.

### Success Story :
### Getting Your Clients to Willingly
### Grow Your Business For You

Although I'm best known as a geek and an Infusionsoft consultant, you don't need technology to attract new business. I've worked with many clients who've successfully used this very strategy to rapidly grow their businesses at minimal cost.

All you need to do is make contact with as many happy clients as possible who you've worked with in the past. Remember, personal contact, either face to face or on the phone, is always significantly more effective than emails. It's also much more likely to win new business!

It's good practice to check in with your past clients from time to time anyway, to refocus them on how good your service has been, and to explore how you can help them achieve more now.

During your conversation, offer them an unmissable incentive to come back to you as a client. This could be a special offer, a bonus, an exclusive gift, or anything else you think will be attractive.

My client, Heidi Strickland-Clark, owner of FastTrack Fit Camp, used this strategy very successfully with...
*Success Story Continued...*

*Success Story Continued...*

...her clients who'd ended their membership. She contacted them personally with a special "three months' membership for the price of two" offer, if they re-joined. This simple strategy increased membership and added £5,000 to her income, in just a couple of days!

I recommend you go one step further. Simply ask your past clients who else they know who might enjoy the same benefits they've enjoyed by working with you. You'll be astounded how many people will be delighted to recommend you, if you only ask.

Top tip— have a surprise "thank you" up your sleeve. Possibly offer them one of your services at no charge or at a specially discounted rate. You'll be delighted just how much additional business this will quickly generate.

Adrian Savage
*Business Consultant and Infusionsoft Expert*
adriansavage.co.uk

But you need to start to feel comfortable about selling anything. You need to feel that you have integrity. You get to choose what you include in your package or programme, so really do some work in terms of thinking about the benefits to your clients, about all the things that they receive by purchasing this product or service. It will have a ripple effect in their life.

For example, let's say somebody buys some weight loss coaching and they lose weight, it doesn't just affect their physical body. It usually affects their opportunities, their mental outlook, their relationships, and their confidence, so really think about all those positive benefits that your ideal clients will get from working with you. Also what happens if they choose not to solve this problem? It doesn't matter whether it's you or someone else, if they choose not to address it, what is the cost of that?

Again, I wouldn't necessarily include this in the conversation. But think through the implications for the person who's ready to take the step with you, if they don't take the step at all. What if they don't get that problem fixed, what is the cost to their lives and their business or whatever environments they're in?

Some really simple stuff that can help is just jotting down all the key elements of your products or service; the features, the advantages, the benefits. Think about what does it cost if they don't get this problem fixed? What are the benefits if they do? Really think about what are all those ripple effects.

Once you've got that mind-set, it's also about thinking that you're doing people a disservice if you don't offer them. Yes, the people in the world need your work, and if you don't offer them what is required, the thing that could help them, it's kind of like you're not giving them their medicine.

Coming from the standpoint of, "I can help you move forward and it's my duty to give you this opportunity," and then it's up to them whether it's a fit.

Okay, so that's the mind-set piece. Now let's go think about some of the structure pieces. These are really simple things that I think we can do when we're caught unaware. For example, when people just phone us and say, "Can you tell me about your service? Can you tell me what you do?"

We can be on the back foot and it's not a great place to be selling from. So what you want to do is set up processes in your business where you schedule your sales calls, even incoming sales calls.

If somebody phones in to enquire about your service, you probably don't want to be taking that call whilst you're on your mobile, driving, or if you don't have your materials on hand.

You need a process where that data is captured, where they get an immediate person to speak to, but then a call is scheduled. So for example, let's say you're a lean management consultant and a company wants to work with you.

They probably send a secretary to phone up and get some general prices and you can have that call sent through to an answering service where they can say, "Yes, we can definitely get all that information for you. We can assess what you need. You could speak with our leads consultant. Can I schedule that in?"

You want somebody to be scheduling your calls in, or you shouldn't promote through your phone service. Even if a customer phones you, you could say, "Yes, I'm with a client at the moment. I would love to help you. Let's schedule a time."

You then have control over that call. It also means the people who are really just time-wasters won't bother to book or are less likely to commit to that, so it will filter a lot of your appointments from the people who perhaps wouldn't be an ideal fit.

Always schedule your sales appointments. You could also do this online by offering a strategy session or a discovery session about your work, or you could just have a 'find out more about working with us' button. That could lead through to an online diary system where people can book in for an appointment.

I use something called Time Trade, but there are lots of other systems, and you can schedule your appointments online there. You just block out the areas that are right for you, the times that are available for you, and people can book it up directly without having to speak to you.

Scheduling your appointment is really important. I also gather some data about people before I speak to them. So in order to book their appointment, they need to have answered a few questions. An example of what they may be signing up for is sales training. In this case the data I'd want to collect might be:

- What are the key outcomes they want to achieve from this training?

- How many people might they need to train?

- What's their budget?

- What are the big innovations going on in their business this year?

So at least you have an idea of what's going on for that client. Also, especially if I'm aiming to see if they are a fit for a high end, high ticket item, I would definitely do some research on the clients.

If you're going to spend half an hour on the call with someone, you want to make it as useful as possible, so just Google them and look at their LinkedIn profile. See what comes up for them or their company so then you have a bit of background knowledge

The next stage is to have a plan and take control of the conversation gently. When you come to actually having your call, have a structure that you work with. It's not just somebody grilling you for prices and trying to get you to prove what you can do, you should very much lead the call.

So you want to start off with a phrase like, "I'm really thrilled to be speaking to you today."

Then you would talk them through how you're going to deliver the call. Depending on your situation, it might be something like, "So what I'll do is because I don't think we've met before, I'll tell you a little bit about my company and myself and how I got to do what I'm doing. I'm going to ask you some questions about your situation so I can find out what the challenges are, and what the things that you most need covered in your business or situation are at the moment, depending on what it is."

Then if it's appropriate, "What I would like to do is make you some recommendations." Then go on to tell them what you will cover, so whatever you've promised in the discovery or strategy session outline, then you definitely want to make sure that you achieve them.

It might be "we will discuss the three ways that you can lose weight by...", or "you can increase your staff retention by...", or "we will look at two strategies that can help you increase your income..." and "...I will give you some resources".

Then if it's appropriate, so basically when they book up for the session, you'll also get information. You can say, "Yes, I do a strategy session that will help you." Then you give them a reason to call: "It will help you to get more income/lose weight/whatever it is."

Then in the call you're building on from that, saying, "So we're going to cover those three things that I promised you, and then if it's appropriate, I'm going to tell you about some ways you can work on a deeper level with me or a more intensive way with my organisation. Would that be okay?"

It's really important that you ask them their permission. Nobody is going to say no, although you might occasionally get someone saying, "Well, I just want to know prices."

You're going to tell them briefly a little bit about yourself or your business, and why you got to do what you're doing. When I work with my clients one-on-one, or in my Conversations That Close programme, we spend a lot of time on just getting that first couple of lines really honed. We give you a complete blueprint of how to make a really powerful impact in your intro without boring prospective clients to death.

We're going to ask them some questions. You're going to start by building some rapport and asking them some questions about their hopes in the area that they want help with. So you might talk a little bit about how things are going for them, chat a little bit about what their market is like, if they're in business.

Start gently asking questions like, "So tell me about what are the biggest challenges you're facing in this area," whichever area it is.

You then want to spend quite a while exploring around what's stopping them achieving the outcome that they want. Then let's paint the picture of what it would look like. So what would you like to achieve in this area?

Let's say it's a company and they're looking to hire someone to help increase staff retention. "So if you have fewer people leaving, what would that look like to you?" "What would be most important as the outcome for you in that area?"

Then you can talk about some details— what are the things that make big impacts with clients in that area, achieving those results?

I would say something like, "So when I work with clients, the things that block them getting to a six-figure income are that they are doing too much work for too little money."

Another reason could be that the branding isn't right.

So let's talk about that, "So those are the three things I want to work with you on. How does that sound?" You just want to make sure people get value from the call from you even if they never work with you again. You want them to come away with a real, positive experience.

Then towards the end, as you get a clear idea of their situation, they've already said you could give them some useful suggestions about their situation. Then you ask them, and collect a little bit more about how, "I would love to share with you about where you can implement this and take it to the next level, work a little deeper with me," or if it's business, I might say, "Is it okay if I tell you about some programmes I really think would help your theme?"

Again, I've never had anyone say no. You just need to be confident when you say that and then I would recommend making one clear proposal. Rather than say, "Well, there's a number of ways we can work. We can do this. We can do that. We can do something else," I would recommend in a one-on-one call, you make one clear proposal.

Something like, "What I recommend to people in your situation is that we spend an entire day together doing a VIP programme and what that will include is…" then you just write it down and bring the conversation back to the fact that it helped them achieve the hopes that they had earlier.

That's the structure of your sales conversation up to this point. You'll then find that they will probably have some questions, so you might say, "Other than the price, which I will come to in a minute, what questions do you have?"

What you want to do is get anything else rather than just

pricing issues dealt with first.

So at the end you can say, "So the investment for this programme is..." then you just want to be quiet. Again, in my Conversations That Close programme, we talk through exactly how to deal with objections, what to do when they are just focused on price. But for most of us, if you just have that clear structure and are really focused on the things that are challenging them most. This is where the call really starts.

This is where people start saying, "Oh, I don't know if my boss would go for that," or "I'm not sure that I can afford that this month," or "I've done a programme before. It didn't get me the results."

This is where you just listen and, coming from a place of it not being attached to the result, you just focus on what things they need and how your programme will support them.

You need to have one clear question. You need to ask for the business. This is again where I see people struggling; they've had a great conversation but they haven't made an offer and they haven't asked for the business. So once you've dealt with the objections, you want to very specifically say, "So how does that sound?", "It sounds like we've covered everything you need to know. When would you like to start?" or "Can we get this booked in?"

Now if this is a small business, they probably have the power and authority to go ahead with that. If it's a larger business you're selling to, like a corporate, then the next step would be, "When would you like me to send you the proposal?" or "Who do I need to speak to?" or "Who do you need to speak to, to get the sign off on this?"

If it's a longer buy-in cycle with a bigger number of decision makers, your job first of all is to find out what the next steps are, what the buying cycle is and how you can help them get this through.

That is a sales conversation, and if you get to that point, you can then schedule another call if it's a corporate sale and it's a longer sales process. So you schedule a call, you write the proposal, you follow up and you do exactly the same process. For most of us, when dealing with small, independent individuals or business to customer sales, you should be able to close it on the call.

Now if they say, "Oh, I would like to think about it," we all have more than enough to think about, I think it's a bit of a disservice leaving people to go away and figure it out for themselves. I would then spend more time with them to say, "That makes sense. But tell me, what are the areas that you're uncertain about?"

You can give them the support then and there and you get a much better chance of getting them to buy while they're on the call, rather than having gone back to their normal life and got in all the key data and then other things get in the way. So your aim is to close them on the call if you can, and for the ones that are not right, we just want a firm yes or a firm, "No, it's not for me." Either is fine. That's absolutely fine.

If it's a no, then you say, "That's fine. Would you like me to keep in touch about other programmes and opportunities that are coming up?" Then again, you know whether to get them on your database or if they're a definite no.

Both of those are great results because you want a handful of clients that are really loyal to you. So that's your sales process for a really effective conversation that closes. Again, if you look at the bonus material for this book on the web, then we will give you some cheat sheets on how to have that conversation.

## Worksheet

*Your sales conversation planning sheet*

How many sales would you need to do to achieve your monthly income goal?

## Now let's look at your conversion rate

What is your usual conversion rate?

If you're not sure put in 20%

## Let's look at inviting people into a sales conversation

How many invitations do you have to make to have 1 sales conversation?

If you're not sure put 3.

Example:

## Now let's look at your conversion rate

If you're not sure put in 20%

**GET CLIENTS FAST**

Let say 10 Clients are needed— 10 to hit your monthly earnings target.

5 out of 10 buy (your sales conversion rate.)

So, you need 20 sales conversations to convert to 10 sales.

**Let's look at inviting people into a sales conversation**

Let's say that you have to make 3 invitations for 1 sales conversation to happen.

No of clients needed

_____  = D

Conversion rate

D x invitation conversion rate = Number of invitations required

So to actually achieve your 10 sales, you'll need invite 60 people into a sales conversation to achieve your target.

# GET SYSTEMATISED

This is about organising your sales system and keeping track of your contact and sales activity. So again, for many of us, selling is not where we came from and it may not be our favourite part of the role.

Actually, being quite methodical and practical about it is probably not a strength for many of us, but it makes a huge difference to know your numbers, to keep track of this stuff— and the good news is you don't need to buy any software. You don't need anything other than a pen and paper, or a spreadsheet if you prefer to work like that.

### Top Tip -
### Inconsistent Marketing Yields Inconsistent Results

Many business owners suffer from the money rollercoaster resulting in inconsistent monthly income. The best way to mitigate this problem is to engage in just 30 minutes of marketing activity each and every day without fail. *Top Tip Continued...*

*...Top Tip Continued*

....You should use this time for outreach activities such as booking speaking engagements, reaching out to past clients, connecting with new clients and finding joint venture partners.

Book this marketing appointment in your calendar now and show up every day to complete the task. You can't grow your business hiding out behind your desk. So reach out daily to find new opportunities. Your business and your bank account will be glad you did.

Julia Felton
*Leader of the Joined Up Business Revolution, aligning leaders, teams and business systems to deliver greater sustainable productivity and profitability*
www.businesshorsepower.com

Some things you're going to want to do are to track how many sales conversations you're having each week and month. Again, that can be a sobering thought because you suddenly realise that you're perhaps not having as many as you would hope.

You want to be tracking how many sales conversations you're having, and you also want to be tracking your conversion rate. Now, if you're a detailed person, you might want to make notes on each of those conversations, so you can learn from them. You could do that in a journal, a Word document, or in a database. There are some great customer relationship management databases, and I recommend one called High-rise, as in the high rise building, High-rise HQ.

But you honestly don't need anything more to start with than a phone, a computer or a notepad, and somewhere you can keep your results. So how many sales calls are you having? What are the results out of, say, 10 calls? How many did you convert? Then some notes on those individual customers which you can keep either in a separate book, or if you have a CRM system then you might want to keep it there.

You also want to look at the average sale per client. What are you selling them and at what price? That's just about being methodical and creating a system where you actually make a call, and you have some time off to just do that little bit of admin. It's not something you should be doing at the end of the week because it will never happen.

The other part of getting systematised is having a plan. If you know that you want to make an extra 50,000 pounds or dollars this year, then you need to look at how many clients we're going to need to sell to and at what price. For example, one of my clients might be on a 5K program, so 10 of those would make a 50K sale, which is fantastic.

So you think, "Wow, so if I've only got to do 10, then what is that for the year? How does that work out?" Let me just explain.

I think you need to focus on your plan: What is your turnover? How many clients at what price do you need to be selling to? Then you do your plan for the year. A 5K sale is more significant and may take more conversions than a 50 pound sale.

Let's say that you need 10 calls to convert one. Some of us may need 20. Some of us may need four. But let's say that it's 10 calls to convert one sale. So over the year we need to be doing 20 lots of that to get our 10 sales.

That's 200 calls over the year. Now that might sound like a lot but that's just under four calls every week! If you're a full time salesperson, you would get that done in a couple of hours. So it's kind of knowing your numbers, and if you go to the online resources with this book, you'll see a template where you can look at:

- How much do you want to earn?

- What do you think is your average closing rate?

- How many calls do you need to have to get to that?

You just work the plan. Once you've planned it, you need to schedule it. This is about putting time in your diary every week for sales activity. So this isn't the marketing, this is just the time when you have your call. This means that you then perhaps block out one or two days a week where you're doing your sales conversations, which is great, because you're then in the zone when you're doing that. You're literally saying, "Right, Mondays and Tuesdays are when I have my sales conversations. That means I can put that in my own diary. It's easy for people to know when they can get hold of me." Then it makes it easier for everyone.

The things you want to do in this system are to track your current stats, and plan your numbers— as in how much you want to earn. What programmes do you want to sell? Or what items do you want to sell? How many of those would you have to sell to make that number?

Then you have to think about your average conversion rate and how many calls, sales conversations, presentations or pitches you're going to have to make to convert those. So let's imagine that, for example, you close one in 10, which is a very low conversion rate. Mine is around one in three, one in four, but I've had a very niche market and a very targeted list. Some of you may get one in 10 to start with, and that is fine, because that still only means you need to do three to four calls a week to get 20 new clients a year.

Let's get these 10 new clients at the premium end. So plan your numbers, schedule your sales time, or your sales call, and then track your results.

Those are the key things, and again if you look at the online resources, we have created some sheets for you where you can track that progress.

## Worksheet

*Annual Sales Planner*

Your income goal for the year

How Will You Achieve This?

| Product/Service | Price | Target No Sales for the Year | Total Income from this Product/ Service |
|---|---|---|---|
|  |  |  |  |

| Product/Service | Price | Target No Sales for the Year | Total Income from this Product/ Service |
|---|---|---|---|
|  |  |  |  |
|  |  |  |  |
|  |  |  |  |
|  |  |  |  |

Visit **www.GetClientsFastBook.com**
For a downloadable version of this spreadsheet

**GET CLIENTS FAST**

Things to think about:

- Which of your products is most profitable?

- Which of your products generates the most income?

- Which have you sold successfully in the past?

*Annual Sales Planner* (EXAMPLE)

Your income goal for the year

How Will You Achieve This?

(Multiply the price by the number of sales to get the total income for each product.)

| Product/Service | Price | Target No Sales for the Year | Total Income from this Product/Service |
|---|---|---|---|
| 1 Day Consultations/ Training | £1500 | 10 | £15000 |

| | | | |
|---|---|---|---|
| High End Client Programmes | £5000 | 10 | £50000 |
| Online Programme 1 | £1000 | 32 | £32000 |
| Online Programme 2 | £300 | 10 | £3000 |
| | | Total | £100000 |

These are now your sales targets.

Visit **www.GetClientsFastBook.com**
For a downloadable version of this spreadsheet

*Sales Call Record*

Week of (insert date)

| Client Name | Date of Call | Result | Next Action |
|---|---|---|---|
| | | | |
| | | | |
| | | | |
| | | | |
| | | | |

Visit **www.GetClientsFastBook.com**
For a downloadable version of this spreadsheet

*Sales Review*

What I did well in my sales conversations this week

What I learned this week

_____

_____

_____

_____

_____

Next steps

_____

_____

_____

_____

_____

Visit **www.GetClientsFastBook.com**
For a downloadable version of this spreadsheet

## *Sales Call Record* (EXAMPLE)

| Client Name | Date of Call | Result | Next Action |
|---|---|---|---|
| Jenny King | 4 Jan | Purchased VIP Day | Send Welcome Pack |
| Paul Smith | 5 Jan | Not ready yet | Book in follow up call in 1 month |
| Millana Jacobs | 5 Jan | Wants to enrol in online programme | Send details of online programme |
| | | | |
| | | | |

---

---

---

---

### Sales Review (EXAMPLE)

**What I did well in my sales conversations this week**

Booked in 3 appointments

Gave a clear offer to each one

**What I learned this week**

I feel uncomfortable asking for the money

**Next steps**

Review how to handle price objections with my coach

---

---

**GET CLIENTS FAST**

_____

_____

_____

_____

_____

_____

## Sales Statistics Record

| Week | No of Sales Calls | No of Sales | Conversion Rate | Total Value of Sales | Average Value of Sales |
|------|-------------------|-------------|-----------------|----------------------|------------------------|
|      |                   |             |                 |                      |                        |
|      |                   |             |                 |                      |                        |

| Week | No of Sales Calls | No of Sales | Conversion Rate | Total Value of Sales | Average Value of Sales |
|---|---|---|---|---|---|
|  |  |  |  |  |  |
|  |  |  |  |  |  |
|  |  |  |  |  |  |
|  |  |  |  |  |  |
|  |  |  |  |  |  |
|  |  |  |  |  |  |

Things to think about:

- Which were your most successful weeks & why?

- Which product or service are you most comfortable selling?

- What factors affect your conversion rate?

Visit **www.GetClientsFastBook.com**
For a downloadable version of this spreadsheet

*Sales Statistics Record* (EXAMPLE)

| Week | No of Sales Calls | No of Sales | Conversion Rate | Total Value of Sales | Average Value of Sales |
|------|-------------------|-------------|-----------------|----------------------|------------------------|
| 1 | 10 | 2 | 20% | 2000 | 1000 |
| 2 | 6 | 2 | 33.3% | 1500 | 500 |
| 3 | 20 | 10 | 50% | 5000 | 500 |

Things to think about:

Which were your most successful weeks & why?

_____

_____

_____

_____

_____

Week 3— I felt I'd had more practice and was 'in the flow.'

Which product or service are you most comfortable selling?

_____

_____

_____

£500 online programme with added coaching.

I feel it represents really good value.

What factors affect your conversion rate?

_____

_____

_____

_____


How many calls I do.

How I'm feeling.

Whether the potential customers have completed a questionnaire.

# GET CLIENTS FOREVER

In this chapter we will look at how to keep you connected to your clients and how to keep adding value, plus some simple keep-in-touch strategies to ensure you are in a great state of mind when they need you again.

This is basic customer service and customer retention. Be that person who is really focused on your client's world, and think about what would be valuable for them. One thing you could do is organise networking meetings.

If it would be useful for them to be in touch with other people in a similar field, or to meet other business owners, then organising networking meetings, like get-togethers, could definitely help. Especially if it's something that is complimentary, or a very low cost item, where people really get to speak to other peers. Or it could be that you arrange for other people to come and speak at those meetings. Be the person that pulls that sort of stuff together, but take it from them - find out from them what would be useful.

## Top Tip -
## Jumpstart Your Success by Hosting a Retreat

We already know that the best way to constantly enrol new clients is not by placing ads or setting up a fancy office, but by developing a loyal community of raving fans. Retreats are a rather overlooked resource when it comes to growing your business. The demand is increasing and their popularity grows in many different industries. Retreats usually combine travel, relaxation, learning, spirituality, networking, activities and personal growth all in one and that's what makes them so appealing.

There are more benefits to running a retreat besides making impact and great income. Because they are usually limited in size, they provide an exclusive environment for creating an intimate, comprehensive rapport with your clients. It makes a perfect opportunity to obtain fantastic testimonials, get referrals, up-sell your high-priced programs and increase influence.

Hosting a retreat does not have to be an overwhelming, stressful process— just the opposite in fact. If you plan it thoroughly it will be the most rewarding event you'll ever create.

*Top Tip Continued...*

*...Top Tip Continued*

There are four phases you need to cover in order to make it run smoothly, and those are:

1. Map out the outline by answering most important questions like why, where, when, what, for whom, how much

2. Prepare content, schedule, inventory and documents

3. Set pricing policy, create marketing plan and start selling

4. Perform the event, over-deliver and have fun

When you set this strategy in place, you will not only make money and build your authority, but also provide tremendous value and an unforgettable experience to your clients.

Sunita Prodan Benolic
*The Passion for Retreats*
www.dreambuildingnow.com

Another thing you can do as a customer retention activity is offer add-on training. Let's say you've delivered a time management course, then you could offer them a complimentary conference call, or an information day or an implementation call. It could be done virtually. It could be a complimentary offering, or it could be something that has a low fee.

Naturally, you want to keep in touch by email or video, sending newsletters and valuable articles; things that are relevant to them. You want to keep in touch with their industry news and finding out what's going on for them. So if your clients are busy mums and they typically have toddlers, you would be wanting to check out those magazines that are relevant to them and just keeping them abreast of anything new that's happening— perhaps new products that are coming out, even though they're not related to you. It's going to be about being a valuable resource to people.

### Top Tip -
### The #1 Mistake Made by Beginning Video Marketers

When most entrepreneurs start doing video marketing, they usually focus on the equipment. Big mistake! Making compelling video is NOT about the equipment. It's about the content— the message.

It's just like cooking. Emeril LeGasse can create a masterful meal with a single hot plate and quality ingredients.... *Top Tip Continued...*

*...Top Tip Continued*

But if you gave me a commercial kitchen, I would produce the same boring meals as always.

Don't buy new equipment! Start with what you have— an iPhone, an old camera, a webcam. If you have no camera, start with screencasting. Focus first on learning the process of creating compelling video, NOT on the equipment!

Lynn Ruby
*Founder of 'Teach Me Video Marketing'*
www.RubyMarketingSystems.com

Send people articles that might be of interest. You might also want to manage how you keep in touch with them on social media. So if you set up Google Alerts with their name, then any time they're mentioned, you'll get notified about it.

If they mention something, like they've won an award, then you can be the first to congratulate them. You also want to keep communicating and finding out about their current issues.

It might be a call, or just a touch-base session. It might be that you send them a survey. But always incentivise them. Think about how to keep abreast of what is important for them.

Finally, it's great to send gifts and holiday promotions— and not just by email. Don't forget to send gifts, treats, small things in the post, it's what we call lumpy mail. Most people don't do this stuff. We rely on email marketing far too much and it can definitely make you stand out if you send a well-chosen and thoughtful gift.

## Worksheet

| Day | Action |
|-----|--------|
| Day 1 | Get a journal or create a new e-document to create your sales planner. |
| Day 2 | Identify one core product or service that you will focus on during the next 30 days. Learn to LOVE this product and get to know it inside out. |

| | |
|---|---|
| | Write a full product overview in your sales planner:<br><br>Who is it for?<br><br>How does it benefit them?<br><br>What is the ONE key pain your product or service can solve?<br><br>What do they lose if they don't purchase this?<br><br>What objections might people say?<br><br>Who are your competitors?<br><br>What is your pricing/package? Any special offers or bonuses? |
| Day 3 | Create or review your marketing materials and admin.<br><br>Are you ready to serve your clients WHEN they say "yes" to a consultation and when they are engaged as a client?<br><br>Check that you have (if relevant): |

| | |
|---|---|
| | Appointment booking system<br><br>(www.timetrade.com)<br><br>Product or service overview sheet/brochure<br><br>Client enrolment form<br><br>Welcome Letter<br><br>Contract<br><br>'Get Started' pack— everything they need to get going<br><br>Welcome gift |
| Day 4 | Check your image & brand<br><br>Does your website, email signature, social media presence etc. reflect your current offering?<br><br>Make sure everything is aligned, so that if someone checks out your website or social media platform, they see that you are an expert in your current offering. |

| | |
|---|---|
| Day 5 | Gather your database. |
| | Make a list of all the potential people you could contact to let them know about what you're offering. |
| | These could include: |
| | Family |
| | Friends |
| | Current & Ex-colleagues |
| | People in associations & clubs you belong to |
| | Your email list/data base |
| | Make sure you have their email and/or postal address |
| Day 6 | Day off— Celebrate your achievements this week! |
| Day 7 | Day off— Plan your next week allowing time for marketing and for having sales conversations/meetings. |

## Week 2

| Day 8 | Practice your sales conversation with a coach or friend, who can take the role of an interested potential client. |
|-------|----------------------------------------------------------------------------------------------------------------------|
|       | Yes, you'll feel daft, but you'll feel much more confident with 'real' clients having been through the process a few times. |
| Day 9 | Create and send a simple email or letter letting people know what you're doing now, and offer the opportunity to schedule a complimentary consultation/meeting with you. (visit our online bonus site **www.GetClientsFastBook.com** for a template) |
|       | Send to half of your contacts. |
|       | For people who have NOT opted in to your database, this should be a personal, solo |
|       | Email and only to people you actually know. Do not add them to your database unless they give you explicit permission. |

| | |
|---|---|
| | Book to attend 3 networking events in the next two weeks.<br><br>Plan your 'elevator pitch' —what you'll say when someone asks "what do you do?"<br><br>Also prepare your 1 minute intro— you may get the opportunity to introduce yourself to the whole room, so plan to tell them about your current service, how it could benefit them and how to go about booking a free consultation/meeting with you.<br><br>(see bonus online content for an example of this at **www.GetClientsFastBook.com**)<br><br>Conduct Sales conversations/Meetings |
| Day 10 | Start booking in Sales conversations/meetings. |
| Day 11 | Send a follow-up reminder email.<br><br>Conduct Sales conversations. |

| | |
|---|---|
| | Review how your sales conversations went with a coach, friend, or mentor.<br><br>Log your sales conversation stats. |
| Day 12 | Day Off! Celebrate your achievements this week. |
| Day 13 | Day Off! Plan your next week including time for sales conversations/meetings and marketing. |
| Day 14 | Create a facebook post offering a taster consultation with you.<br><br>(see bonus online content for an example facebook post at **www.GetClientsFastBook.com**) |

## Week 3

| Day 15 | Conduct Sales meetings/conversations. |
|---|---|
| Day 16 | Attend a networking event.<br><br>Offer an invitation into a free consultation/meeting. |
| Day 17 | Send a reminder email (yes, really) to anyone who hasn't replied to your earlier email.<br><br>Post again on Facebook. |
| Day 18 | Attend a networking event.<br><br>Conduct sales conversations/meetings.<br><br>Follow up Facebook messages.<br><br>Review your sales conversations and log your figures. |

| | |
|---|---|
| Day 19 | Day Off! Celebrate your achievements this week. |
| Day 20 | Day Off! Plan your next week including time for sales conversations/meetings and marketing. |
| Day 21 | Send a simple email or letter letting people know what you're doing now, and offer the opportunity to schedule a complimentary consultation/meeting with you, to the 2nd half of your list (visit our online bonus site **www.GetClientsFastBook.com** for a template.)<br><br>Conduct sales calls/meetings. |

## Week 4

| | |
|---|---|
| Day 22 | Post an invitation to a free consultation/meeting your LinkedIn contacts. |

| Day 23 | Conduct sales conversations/meetings. |
|--------|----------------------------------------|
| Day 24 | Attend a networking event. |
| Day 25 | Conduct sales calls/meetings. |
| Day 26 | Conduct sales calls/meetings. Follow up with LinkedIn contacts. |
| Day 27 | Day off! Relax! |
| Day 28 | Day off— Plan your week ahead. |

| | |
|---|---|
| Day 29 | Review your campaign— see our bonus content online to get access to a sales campaign review sheet: **www.GetClientsFastBook.com** |
| Day 30 | Celebrate your success!<br><br>Let me know how you got on our Facebook group.<br><br>Plan your next 30 day sales goal! |

# **NEXT STEPS**

## Need a Little Help?

Now is the time to implement and get things done.

If you're like me, you may be 'high' for a few days on your new found sales skills, and excited about making it all happen.

However, then the dog gets sick, a client project goes wrong, your time disappears and your fabulous plans get derailed.

When you go back to rekindling your love affair with sales, the flame is not burning so brightly, and some sneaky fears start to creep in, keeping you stuck or spinning your wheels. I know, I've been there.

That can be really disheartening, and can make you doubt yourself and your business.

This is when you need to surround yourself with a super strong support team, and have a clear plan of exactly what to do next, so you can banish feelings of overwhelm, and have the courage to do the scary stuff that will make all the difference.

So if you need a little extra help, I'd love to invite you to join my powerful community of awesome, 'ordinary' entrepreneurs at my Get Clients Fast Intensive.

## The Get Clients Fast Intensive

This action-orientated programme will take you through the entire Get Clients Fast process, giving you the support and structure to get your sales strategy done NOW!

What this system means for you is that you will know EXACTLY what to do to enroll lots of new clients, anytime you wish. No "perfect" niche, website or business cards required.

Imagine feeling so secure in knowing that you can create cash flow whenever you need it, or WANT the cash to easily pay down debt, indulge in a retreat or spa day, take a holiday, or add to your family's savings plan.

Fabulous, right? YES and... make no mistake, while this system IS simple, it's also life-changing.

Because what you'll learn is mission critical for your business at ANY stage. You'll use the principles to get your first or next client, and over and over again as you get your next 100 clients... and beyond.

I've used the principles of this system to build several successful businesses and generate consistent multiple four & five figure paydays.

Not only can this system help you bring in massive amounts of revenue lightning fast.

But it's something ANYONE can do.

How do I know?

Because here's the truth— I started from zero.

**This new approach has...**

Stopped me sinking HOURS into strategy sessions, only to hear, "Sounds great, but... I can't afford it."

Tripled my closing rate & brought a massive increase in sales.

Built my confidence and credibility, and helped me serve more people than ever before.

Helped me grow a secure International Client Base, giving me the freedom to work wherever I choose.

---

### Success Story

This week I started having sales conversations using the process you showed me. I did two calls and was prepared for the usual money objection, but it didn't come! .....First time ever! I pitched the mastery program at $2884 to both. One said **yes** and has already paid in full, the other has paid a 50% deposit! That's the most I've ever made in one month, let alone one day!

Jane Simmonds
*Natural Health Expert*

---

## Are You Ready For New Clients Now?

I'll show you how to implement the exact step-by-step 'Get Clients Fast' process I used to turn around my company and attract high paying clients from around the globe.

In fact, this is the only training I know of that gives you ALL THREE critical elements you need to be successful with sales consultations:

### (1) A Step-By-Step System for Consultations That Leads To "Yes"

You will have a proven step-by-step system that you can follow during each and every time you have a consultation with a potential client. In fact, I'll give you a detailed script that shows you exactly what to do at every step of your consultation. No more guessing, fumbling and fear of rejection during your initial consultations.

## (2) A Training Programme for Getting All the Consultations (And Clients) You Want

You'll discover new strategies and step-by-step methods designed to help attract as many one-on-one consultations as you want. The more consultations you have, the more clients you'll be able to enroll, using the Conversations That Close system for conducting consultations that lead to YES.

## (3) The Tools to Transform Your Inner Game and Build Your Confidence

If you dread holding complimentary consultations, if the thought of "selling" your services makes you uncomfortable...

And if you're ready to have a breakthrough, then my Get Clients Fast programme includes bonus tools designed to help you step into a whole new level of confidence!

It's the only course that takes you by the hand and walks you, step-by-step, through everything you need to transform your life and your business with short but meaningful conversations.

I've just revamped this Bestselling training program with YOU in mind, to solve YOUR biggest challenges when it comes to "getting out there" to get clients.

---

### Success Story

"My confidence is soaring, and *my sales closing rate has gone from 1 in 12 to 1 in 5* since working with Helen."

Natalie Sullivan
www.facebook.com/natalierecommends

---

### Client-Getting Challenge No. 1: OVERWHELM

---

I know you're overwhelmed with to-do's, especially with "shiny new marketing objects" on the scene (read: Twitter, Facebook, infographics, video, and on and on). That's why in my Get Clients Fast , I lay out a super-simple path to follow, consisting of ONLY what you really need right now.

## Client-Getting Challenge No. 2: TIME

You're juggling work, being a partner, kids and Goodness knows what else. I know because I am, too! So I've designed the action steps in The Get Clients Fast Intensive to take the least amount of time possible.

## Client-Getting Challenge No. 3: MONEY

If you're like I was back in the day, you may have to create the money to invest in the advanced trainings you want. And "marketing budget?" —hmmm, haven't seen that in a while. That's why nearly ALL of the strategies in The Get Clients Fast Intensive are free— and the others are low cost.

## Client-Getting Challenge No. 4: DROWING IN DECISION-MAKING

Website, logo, tag line, what to offer, who to serve... and for women, picking a niche can be one of the most agonizing decisions of all. Which is why in the Get Clients Fast Intensive, we'll cut through the clutter and make decisions EASY. (And you won't have to pick a niche to start getting clients.

> **Client-Getting Challenge No. 5: FOCUS**

Do you ever get to the end of the week, knowing you've worked really hard, but you're not sure what you've accomplished? Yep, me too— without a plan, I'm useless.

I love a paint by numbers system, so my 30-day action guide lays out the steps, day by day, to get clients. So you know exactly what to do when you sit down at your desk in the morning. (Weekends are off!)

> **Client-Getting Challenge No. 6:**
> **WHERE TO <u>FIND</u> CLIENTS (who happily pay your fees)**

Great news: your clients are in your world already! I'll walk you through an extensive list of the best places to find clients right now, PLUS give you the key mindset shifts that make these hidden opportunities visible.

## Client-Getting Challenge No. 7: THE "INNER GAME"

When you put yourself out there, you're gonna hit your edge. You can have all the client-getting strategies in the world, but without proven tools to transform and move through your fear, you'll stay stuck. So I'm sharing exactly how I've up-leveled my BE-ing to go from barely earning 10k in a year to consistent $20k+ months.

### Success Story

"Already after **two weeks in** the programme I've managed to speak to more people than the last two months, and have **closed two clients**. I cannot describe the impact it will have in my business— I have a system now that I know works**."**

Konstantinos Kapelas, MSc
*Founder: Kapelas Health & Vitality SystemTM*
www.totalhealthnow.co.uk

## Training When & Where You Want It

You can access this programme from anywhere in the world, at a time that suits you. Each week I will walk you through the simple steps you need to take to prepare for and create powerful client enrolling conversations and give you the tools to start enrolling clients from where you are with what you've got!

So are you ready to finally master the art of attracting clients and generating income in your business?

Everything you want to create in your life begins with one thing— a decision.

If you're reading this, you're ready. So let's get you started right now...

Just visit

**www.GetClientsFastTraining.Com**

And join our community of thriving entrepreneurs

# Want to be a 'Hel's Angel'?

One of the key ways I've grown my business over the last few years is by connecting with like-minded entrepreneurs and creating joint venture or affiliate relationships with them.

I'm also an active affiliate partner for some of the biggest names in the industry, and affiliate commission accounts for approximately 20% of my turnover.

I now have a thriving community of affiliate partners, affectionately known as 'Hel's Angels', who I LOVE sending MONEY to on a regular basis.

That's right.

If you tell your colleagues, friends, subscribers, and customers about any of my programs or services, and they purchase through your affiliate links, we'll pay you a generous 20-50% affiliate referral commission (depending on the product).

My team will do all the order processing. You just sit back and collect your payments.

There is NO limit to the number of people you can get commissions for!

Here are some ways you can promote us:

- In your newsletter

- In your e-zine
- On your website

- On your website's links page

- In editorial coverage on your website

- In advertising slots on your website

- In conversations with friends and colleagues

- At networking and lead generation meetings in your town

If you'd like to learn more about becoming a Hel's Angel, just visit the website below:

**www.PartnerWithHelen.Com**

## A Note from Helen...

Dear Awesome Entrepreneur,

Congratulations, you did it! You put time and energy to go through the entire book and create your fantastic sales plan.

Most business books end up half-read gathering dust on the shelf, so I'm so proud that you've got this far.

You've set the wheels in motion for your goals to come true, your business to thrive and your life to become less stressful and more vibrant, knowing that you have a consistent stream of ideal clients.

Just remember, the more you revisit this book, the more intimate you become with these special goals and plans of yours, and the faster they will happen.

Schedule your actions in your calendar NOW and start TODAY!

Remember, we're looking for progress, not perfection. By following the process in this book, you're setting yourself up for increased productivity, prosperity, and purpose in your business.

I believe in you and your dreams, so let's make some of those amazing dreams happen!

Here's to your success!

Helen Vandenberghe